Vegetai ... Cookbook

Easy and Tasty Vegetarian Slow Cooker Recipes

Table of Contents

Introduction

Times have certainly changed. People, all around the world, live a fast-paced life to keep up with the demands of the new generation. With everyone so focused on earning a living, most households have both mothers and fathers work full-time jobs just to sustain the monthly expenses of the family. And although it is good progress for mothers to be equally competing in their respective fields with men, it is also true that time spent with family especially with children is compromised. Gone are the days when mothers have time to prepare meals and have enough time to spend in the kitchen cooking the family's supper. Fortunately together with changing times, technological advancements have helped eased the problems created by this fast-paced world we all presently live in. Nowadays, many kitchen appliances are readily available and affordable to aid parents in preparing quick, yet healthy vegetarian meals for their families. One of the many kitchen appliances that can be the solution to this present issue is the slow cooker.

Slow cookers have actually been existing in the market for decades. Although its popularity has not really reached all households at the onset of its release in the 1970s, it has definitely eased its way in the present day kitchen because it is turning out to be a necessity for busy moms. Slow cookers may ironically take hours to prepare sumptuous, healthy vegetarian meals for the family but its convenient usage stems from not having to watch over the meal that it cooks.

Aside from the convenience of using a slow cooker, there are actually scientific evidences that show that slow cooking has many advantages that promote good health. One of the many health benefits of slow cooking is retaining the good nutrients of the vegetarian ingredients. It is tested and proven that cooking over low heat does not exhaust the nutrients of most ingredients. High heat or quick cooking using expend all good nutrients present in, for example, vegetables. Meals that are quickly and hastily prepared may be left undercooked which may transmit bacteria like e-coli or salmonella. Slow cooked meals definitely eliminate those risks.

Convinced enough? Purchase your own slow cooker and start preparing the many slow cooked vegetarian recipes in this book. These meals are extensive as the recipes are famous meals from various parts of the world. Take a journey around the world by preparing slow cooked meals presented in this recipe book. Your family will definitely enjoy these vegetarian recipes.

Pumpkin and Peanut Soup
(Makes 5 servings - Cook Time: 6 hours)

Ingredients:

- 500 g. pumpkin, peeled and cubed

- 1 tbsp. olive oil

- 1 white onion, diced

- 2 cloves garlic, minced

- 3 c. vegetable broth

- 3 pcs. Serrano chili, chopped

- 1 small knob ginger, minced

- 1 tsp. allspice powder

- 1 c. tomato juice

- ½ c. organic peanut butter

- Salt and pepper to taste

- Fresh parsley for garnish

Directions:

1. Sauté the garlic, onions, and ginger in a non-stick pan. After a couple of minutes, turn off the heat.

2. Place all the ingredients, including the sautéed vegetables, in a slow cooker. Cook over low heat for 6 hours.

3. Transfer the coarse soup to a blend, a batch at a time. Whiz until it turns into a smooth mixture.

4. Serve in a bowl topped with chopped parsley.

Sopa de Ajo (Garlic Soup)
(Makes 6 servings - Cook Time: 8 hours)

Ingredients:

- ¼ c. olive oil

- 1 white onion, diced

- 4 bulbs garlic, peeled and separated in cloves

- 6 c. vegetable broth

- 1 lemon, juice

- 1 tomato, diced

- 1 c. feta cheese

- 1 c. croutons

- 2 stalks green onions, chopped

- Salt and pepper to taste

Directions:

1. Combine the oil, onion, and garlic in the slow cooker, cook these on low for 5 hours.

2. Add in the vegetable broth and cook for a couple more hours.

3. Transfer the mixture to a blender and pulse until smooth. Place back into the slow cooker. Add the lemon juice, salt, and pepper.

4. Serve in a bowl topped with tomatoes, feta cheese, and croutons.

Bean and Vegetable Clear Soup
(Makes 4 servings -   Cook Time: 5 hours)

Ingredients:

- ½ kilo dry white beans

- 2 stalks celery, chopped

- 1 c. broccoli florets, chopped

- 1 red onion, chopped

- 4 cloves garlic, minced

- 2 large carrots, peeled and diced

- 1 tsp. fennel seeds

- 2 tsp. oregano powder

- ¼ tsp. red pepper flakes

- 5 c. vegan broth

- Salt and pepper to taste

Directions:

1. Place all the ingredients in a slow cooker. Cook on high for 5 hours. Check if the beans are already tender before serving.

2. Serve in individual bowls. Enjoy.

Yummy Corn Chowder

(Makes 5 servings - Cook Time: 7 hours)

Ingredients:

- 2 tbsp. corn oil

- 1 large white onion, coarsely chopped

- 1 large red bell pepper, cored and diced

- 2 large russet potatoes, peeled and diced

- 2 cans sweet corn kernels with brine

- 2 ½ c. vegan broth

- 1 tsp. cumin powder

- ½ tsp. Spanish paprika

- 1 c. almond milk

- Salt and pepper to taste

- Chopped green onions for garnish

Directions:

1. Sauté the onions in corn oil until it turns translucent. Transfer onions to slow cooker.

2. Add all the ingredients, except for the green onions, in the slow cooker.

3. Cook on low for 7 hours.

4. Transfer the soup to a blender and pulse until it forms a smooth chowder.

5. Serve and enjoy.

Hearty Mung Bean Soup
(Makes 5 servings - Cook Time:9 hours)

Ingredients:

- ½ kilo yellow mung beans, washed and drained

- 2 stalks celery, chopped

- 6 stalks green onions, chopped

- 2 large carrots, peeled and diced

- 2 cloves garlic, minced

- 1 red onion, diced

- 6 c. vegan broth

- 1 bay leaf

- Salt and pepper to taste

- 2 tbsp. sesame oil for serving

Directions:

1. Combine all the ingredients in a slow cook. Cook on low heat for 9 hours or until the beans are tender.

2. Place in individual bowls. Drizzle over sesame oil before serving.

Taro Soup

(Makes 5 servings - Cook Time: 5 hours)

Ingredients:

- 1 kilo fresh taro, peeled, washed and cubed

- 1 white onion, diced

- 4 cloves garlic, minced

- 2 stalks celery, chopped

- 5 c. vegan broth

- 1 c. almond milk

- 1 tsp. tarragon leaves

- 2 c. water cress

- Salt and pepper to taste

- ½ c. toasted slivered almonds, for garnish

Directions:

1. Combine the vegan broth, taro, onions, celery, and garlic in a slow cooker. Cook on high heat for 5 hours or until taro is tender.

2. If taro is tender, turn off heat. Pour in the milk and add the seasonings. Mix well.

3. Transfer the soup to a blender and whiz until smooth.

4. Transfer to a large bowl. While the soup is piping hot, add the water cress. Stir gently.

5. Serve in individual bowls topped with almonds. Enjoy.

Caribbean Black Bean Soup
(Makes 4 servings - Cook Time: 7 hours)

Ingredients:

- ½ kilo black bean, washed and drained

- 2 red onions, diced

- 1 large carrot, peeled and diced

- 1 c. diced fire roasted tomatoes

- 1 c. crushed tomatoes

- 1 Caribbean pepper, seeded and chopped

- 1 yellow capsicum, cored, seeded, and chopped

- 1 red bell pepper, cored, seeded, and chopped

- 1 sprig cilantro, chopped

- 1 ½ tbsp. cumin powder

- 1 tsp. cayenne powder

- ½ tsp. Sriracha

- 4 cloves garlic, minced

- 1 bay leaf

- 2 c. water

- Sea salt and pepper to taste

Directions:

1. Place the washed black bean in a basin and soak with 2 cups of water overnight.

2. Drain and rinse the black beans. Combine the beans with tomatoes, garlic, onion, 4 cups of water, salt, pepper, cumin, cayenne, sriracha, bay leaf, and Caribbean pepper in the slow cooker. Cover over high heat for 4 hours.

3. Add the carrots, cilantro, capsicum, and bell pepper. Season with salt and pepper again. Put the heat to low and cook for 2 hours.

4. Serve in a bowl with a dollop of sour cream.

Vegetarian Rigatoni Soup
(Makes 5 servings - Cook Time: 7 hours)

Ingredients:

- 1 white onion, diced

- 1 c. fresh button mushrooms, halved

- 1 zucchini, peeled and diced

- 2 cloves garlic, minced

- ½ c. tomato sauce

- 1 c. diced tomatoes, in can

- 3 c. vegan broth

- 1 bay leaf

- 1 tsp. oregano powder

- ½ tbsp. dried basil leaves

- 2 c. fresh kale leaves

- 200 g. rigatoni noodles (cooked according to package instructions)

- Salt and pepper to taste

- Fresh basil leaves for garnish

Directions:

1. Place all ingredients, except for the garnish and pasta, in a slow cooker. Cook on low heat for 7 hours.

2. After 6 ½ hours, cook the rigatoni noodles in a medium casserole according to package instructions.

3. Add the noodles to the soup after the timer's done.

4. Serve in individual bowls topped with fresh basil leaves

Red Bean Soup
(Makes 4 servings - Cook Time: 11 hours)

Ingredients:

- ½ kilo dry red beans, washed and soaked in water for 5 hours

- 1 white onion, diced

- 1 red bell pepper, cored and diced

- 4 c. vegan broth

- 3 cloves garlic, minced

- 1 bay leaf

- ½ tbsp. cumin powder

- Salt and pepper to taste

- Chopped fresh coriander for garnish

Directions:

1. Place all the ingredients, except for the coriander, in a slow cooker. Cook over low heat for 11 hours or until the red beans are tender.

2. Transfer the soup in a blender and pulse until it turns smooth.

3. Serve in individual bowls topped with chopped coriander.

Favorite Mac and Three Cheese
(Makes 5 servings - Cook Time: 5 hours)

Ingredients:

- 2 c. campanelle or rigatoni pasta, raw

- 2 c. cheddar cheese, cubed

- 5 c. full cream milk

- 4 tbsp. butter

- ½ c. grated parmesan cheese

- ½ c. grated mozzarella cheese

- 1 c. heavy cream

- 1 tbsp. garlic powder

- Salt and pepper to taste

Directions:

1. Place the raw pasta at the bottom of the slow cooker. Place over the cheddar cheese and milk. Finally, add the butter and seasonings.

2. Slow cook on high for an hour and then reduce to low and cook for another 4 hours. Before serving the dish, sprinkle over the parmesan and mozzarella plus the heavy cream. Mix well.

3. Serve and enjoy.

Vegetarian Punjabi Treat with a Twist
(Makes 4 servings - Cook Time: 2 hours)

Ingredients:

- 1 large zucchini, diced

- 1 large yellow potato, diced

- 1 thumb-size ginger, grated

- 6 cloves garlic, minced

- 1 tbsp. cumin powder

- 1 tsp. red chili powder

- 1 tbsp. masala paste

- 1 tbsp. Serrano chili, chopped

- ¼ c. coconut oil

- Salt and pepper to taste

- Fresh coriander to taste

Directions:

1. In a slow cooker, mix the zucchini, potato, onion, garlic, Serrano chili, ginger, cumin, chili powder, masala, turmeric, and coconut oil. Use a wooden spoon to gently mix the ingredients, making sure that the spices infuse the vegetables. Cook these over high heat for an hour.

2. After an hour, use the wooden spoon to mix the vegetables again, this time making sure it doesn't stick at the bottom of the pot. Cook on medium heat for another hour.

3. After the second hour, check if there is too much moisture in the mix. If it does cook it on low for another half hour. Sprinkle over the salt and fresh coriander.

4. Serve and enjoy.

Delicious Black Bean Dip
(Makes 10 servings - Cook Time: 3 hours)

Ingredients:

- ½ package cream cheese, room temperature

- ½ package quick melting cheese, grated

- 1 c. sour cream

- 1 tsp. cumin

- 1 tsp. Spanish paprika

- ½ tsp. oregano powder

- 2 c. cheddar cheese, grated

- ½ c. full cream milk

- 1 large can refried bean

Directions:

1. Place the cream cheese, melting cheese, refried beans, cheddar cheese, milk, spices, and sour cream in a slow cooker. Cook on low heat for 3 hours. Mix occasionally.

2. Check the consistently once in a while. Serve with a bowl of nachos. Enjoy.

Couscous with Vegetables
(Makes 6 servings - Cook Time: 5 hours)

Ingredients:

- 2 tbsp. canola oil

- 2 white onion, diced

- 2 cloves garlic, minced

- 1 small zucchini, diced

- 1 large carrot, peeled and diced

- 1 can chickpeas, washed and drained

- 1 tsp. turmeric powder

- 1 tsp. cumin powder

- 1 green bell pepper, seeded and diced

- 1 red bell pepper, seeded and diced

- 2 sprigs coriander, chopped

- 2 tomatoes, seeded and diced

- 3 c. vegetable broth

- 1 tbsp. honey

- 1 lemon, juice

- 2 c. couscous

- 1 tbsp. extra virgin olive oil

- Salt and pepper to taste

Directions:

1. On a non-stick pan, sauté the onions and garlic in canola oil. Once the onions become translucent, add the cumin and turmeric. Season with salt and pepper. Transfer these to the slow cooker. Add the other vegetables except the coriander leaves. Add the water and honey too. Season again. Cook on low heat for 5 hours.

2. After 5 hours, place the raw couscous in a large mixing bowl. Get about 2 cups of boiling broth from the slow cooker and pour these over the couscous. Drizzle some extra virgin oil and lemon juice. Stir and cover for a couple of minutes. Once the water is sucked by the couscous, remove the cover and use a pair of forks to fluff it.

3. Serve the couscous with the vegetables as siding.

Couscous Enchilada
(Makes 5 servings - Cook Time: 5 hours)

Ingredients:

- 1 can black beans, washed and drained

- 1 can whole kernel corn, washed and drained

- 2 cans red enchilada sauce

- 1 can fire roasted tomatoes

- 1 tbsp. sliced jalapenos

- 1 c. raw couscous

- 1 c. vegan broth, boiled

- 2 oz. sour cream

- 2 oz. light cream cheese

- Salt and pepper to taste

- 1 c. grated cheddar cheese

- 2 large tomatoes, chopped

- 1 avocado, diced

- 1 tbsp. fresh coriander, chopped

Directions:

1. Place all ingredients, except for the coriander, chopped tomatoes, and diced avocado, in the slow cooker. Stir the ingredients using a wooden spoon.

2. Sprinkle the grated cheese over the mixture. Cook on low heat for 5 hours or until the beans are tender.

3. Serve on a plate with a side of tomatoes, coriander, and avocados.

Baba Ganoush (Slow Cooked Eggplant)

(Makes 1 serving - Cook Time: 4 hours)

Ingredients:

- 2 medium eggplant, whole, washed and poked with a fork

- 2 cloves garlic, whole

- 1 lemon, juice

- 2 tbsp. sesame seed paste

- 1 sprig fresh parsley, washed and chopped

- 1 tsp. roasted sesame seeds

- 1 tbsp. extra virgin olive oil

- 2 tbsp. kalamata olives, sliced

- Salt and pepper to taste

Directions:

1. Make sure the whole eggplants are poked by a fork several times on all sides.

2. Places the eggplants in the slow cooker. Cook over high heat for 2 hours.

3. After 2 hours, remove the eggplant using tongs. Cut the eggplants in half, lengthwise. Remove as much seeds as possible. Remove the skin as well. Using a masher or fork, mash the eggplants.

4. Transfer the mashed eggplants to a food processor. Add the sesame paste, garlic, lemon juice, salt, and pepper. Drizzle some olive oil. Pulse until it forms a smooth dip.

5. Serve on a plate surrounded by sliced kalamata olives. Drizzle some oil and sprinkle over the roasted sesame seeds.

6. Serve with some pita bread.

Eggplant Lasagna
(Makes 6 servings - Cook Time: 8 hours)

Ingredients:

- 1 tbsp. olive oil

- 1 bottle pomodoro sauce

- 4 medium eggplant, washed and cut into thin slices

- 9 lasagna noodles, cut to fit slow cooker

- 1 can cream of mushroom

- 2 c. mozzarella cheese, grated

- Salt and pepper to taste

- Chopped fresh basil for topping

Directions:

1. Brush the slow cooker with olive oil. Get a half cup of pomodoro sauce and place at the bottom of the pot. Place the lasagna noodles to cover the bottom of pot. Place ¼ cup of cream of mushroom over the noodles, a layer of sliced eggplant, and a ½ cup of pomodoro sauce. Repeat the process to make 3 layers.

2. For the final layer, place the grated mozzarella cheese with a bit of pomodoro sauce on top.

3. Cover the slow cooker and cook on low for 6 hours.

4. After 6 hours, let the lasagna stay inside the slow cooker for another hour to set.

5. Slice and serve topped with fresh basil.

Healthy Vegetarian Omelette
(Makes 4 servings - Cook Time: 2 hours)

Ingredients:

- 6 organic eggs
- ½ c. skim milk
- 1 tsp. minced garlic
- 1 c. broccoli florets
- 1 green bell pepper, seeded and thinly sliced
- 2 small onions, finely chopped
- Salt and pepper to taste
- Pinch of chili powder for heat
- 2 tbsp. Monterey jack cheese, grated

- 2 tomatoes, diced

- 1 tbsp. olive oil

- fresh spring onions for garnish

Directions:

1. Grease the slow cooker with olive oil. Cover and turn on heat, keep it at low.

2. On a mixing bowl, beat the eggs. Add the milk, salt, half of the minced garlic, pepper, and chili powder. Beat well.

3. Add the broccoli, bell pepper, half of the onions and the rest of the garlic to the egg mixture. Beat well again.

4. Transfer the egg mix to the slow cooker. Increase the heat to high and cook for 1 hour. Check after an hour if the egg are cooked. If not, add another 30 minutes.

5. Once the eggs are done, sprinkle over the grated cheese. Let it cook for another 10 minutes.

6. Serve the omelette on a plate. Sprinkle over the spring onions.

Button Mushroom Stroganoff

(Makes 3 servings - Cook Time: 3 hours)

Ingredients:

- 1 can sliced mushrooms, drained

- ½ c. mushroom brine, from the sliced mushrooms

- 1 can cream of mushroom

- 3 cloves garlic, minced

- 1 onions, finely chopped

- 2 tsp. smoked paprika powder

- Salt and pepper to taste

- Fresh parsley for garnish

Directions:

1. Place all the ingredients except for the parsley in the slow cooker. Cook over high heat for 3 hours. Stir every 30 minutes to avoid burning the mushrooms.

2. Serve over a plate of pasta or rice.

Three-Kinds Mushroom Stroganoff

(Makes 4 servings - Cook Time: 8 hours)

Ingredients:

- 300 g. button mushrooms, halved

- 200 g. Portobello mushrooms, sliced

- 300 g. oyster mushrooms, sliced

- 6 cloves garlic, minced

- 1 large white onion, thinly sliced

- 2 c. vegan broth

- ½ c. almond milk

- 2 tsp. Spanish paprika

- 1 tbsp. sour cream

- Salt and pepper to taste

- Fresh green onions, for garnish

Directions:

1. Put the mushrooms, garlic, onion, vegan broth, almond milk, and paprika in a slow cooker. Cook on low for 8 hours.

2. After 8 hours, add the sour cream, salt and pepper. Stir well.

3. Serve on a bowl of rice or cooked pasta. Garnish with green onions.

Vegetarian Minestrone
(Makes 8 servings - Cook Time: 7 hours)

Ingredients:

- 1 zucchini, cubed

- 1 carrot, cubed

- 2 stalks celery, chopped

- 1 white onion, chopped

- 1 clove garlic, minced

- 2 c. vegetable broth

- 2 c. tomato juice

- ½ c. button mushrooms, drained

- 1 tbsp. dried basil

- ½ tsp. oregano powder

- ½ can diced tomatoes

- 1 c. raw elbow macaroni

- Salt and pepper to taste

- 2 tbsp. pecorino romano cheese, grated

Directions:

1. Place all the ingredients in the slow cooker except for the elbow macaroni and cheese. Cover over low heat for 6 hours.

2. After 6 hours, stir in the pasta. Cook for another 30 minutes over high heat.

3. Serve on a bowl. Sprinkle over the grated cheese.

Chickpeas and Quinoa Chili
(Makes 6 servings - Cook Time: 8 hours)

Ingredients:

- 1 white onion, finely chopped

- 3 garlic cloves, minced

- 1 stalk celery, chopped

- 1 red bell pepper, seeded and diced

- 1 green bell pepper, seeded and diced

- 1 can crushed tomatoes

- 4 c. vegetable broth, low sodium

- 1 c. chick peas, drained

- ½ c. brine from chick peas

- 1 can pinto beans

- 2 tbsp. chili powder

- 2 tsp. cumin powder

- 1 tbsp. oregano powder

- ½ raw quinoa

Directions:

1. Combine all ingredients in the slow cooker. Cook over low heat for 8 hours.

2. Serve with a platter of nachos or lettuce leaves.

Vegetarian Frittata

(Makes 5 servings - Cook Time: 2 ½ hours)

Ingredients:

- 2 c. artichoke hearts, quartered

- 2 c. roasted red bell peppers, diced

- 1 red onion, sliced thinly

- 8 organic eggs, beaten

- 1 c. Monterey jack cheese

- ½ tsp. garlic powder

- 1 tsp. Italian seasoning

- Salt and pepper to taste

- Fresh green onions, for garnish

Directions:

1. Place the beaten eggs in a slow cooker.

2. Carefully add the artichokes, peppers, onion, and other seasonings in the slow cooker. Use a wooden spoon to stir the ingredients.

3. Once the mixture settles, sprinkle over the shredded Monterey Jack cheese.

4. Cook on low for 2 ½ hours.

5. Serve with a garnish of chopped green onions.

Tofu and Lima Beans Curry

(Makes 6 servings - Cook Time: 6 hours)

Ingredients:

- 1 c. taro, peeled and cubed

- 1 c. sweet potato, peeled and cubed

- 2 c. artichoke hearts, chopped coarsely

- 1 white onion, diced

- 1 tbsp. curry powder

- 1 tbsp. brown sugar

- 1 small knob ginger, minced

- 1 c. lima beans, peeled, soaked and rinsed

- 1 can diced tomatoes, in can

- 1 can coconut milk

- 1 pack firm tofu, drained, dried, and cubed

- 2 tbsp. palm oil

- Salt and pepper to taste

Directions:

1. Place all ingredients, except the tofu and the palm oil, in a slow cooker. Stir all the ingredients making sure it is evenly distributed. Cook on low for 5 hours.

2. Dry the tofu using paper towels. Pan fry the tofu cubes on a non-stick pan using the palm oil. Turn off heat once the tofu turns brown. Set aside.

3. Add the cooked tofu in the slow cooker once the timer is done. Cook on low for another half an hour.

4. Serve with a side of steamed rice or flat bread.

Stuffed Bell Peppers
(Makes 4 servings - Cook Time: 5 hours)

Ingredients:

- 4 large whole bell peppers (either green, red, or yellow), tops sliced off and seeded

- 1 c. raw couscous

- 1 can white beans, washed and rinsed

- 1 can refried beans

- 1 ½ c. store-bought salsa

- 1 tsp. cumin powder

- 1 tsp. chili powder

- 1 tsp. onion powder

- 1 tsp. garlic powder

- 1 c. grated mozzarella

- Salt and pepper to taste

- ½ c. vegan broth

- 2 tbsp. fresh coriander, chopped (for garnish)

- Lime wedges (as siding)

Directions:

1. Using a mixing bowl, mix the raw couscous, beans, salsa, powdered spices, salt and pepper. Spoon the mixture into each bell pepper.

2. Pour ½ cup vegan broth to the bottom of the slow cooker. Place the prepared bell peppers in the slow cooker, slightly dipped on the broth. Cook on low heat for 4 ½ hours or until the bell peppers are tender.

3. Sprinkle over the mozzarella cheese over each bell pepper and cook for another half hour or until it melts.

4. Serve on a platter garnished with freshly chopped coriander and lime wedges.

Stewed Vegetables in Curry Sauce

(Makes 4 servings - Cook Time: 8 hours)

Ingredients:

- 1 tsp. canola oil

- 1 white onion, diced

- 1 medium sweet beet, peeled, washed, and diced

- 1 medium red potato, peeled, washed, and diced

- 1 tbsp. curry powder

- 1 tbsp. brown sugar

- 1 small knob ginger, grated

- 3 cloves garlic, minced

- 2 c. vegan broth

- 2 can Great Northern Beans, washed and drained

- 1 green bell pepper, diced

- 1 red bell pepper, diced

- 1 medium head cauliflower, chopped

- 1 can crushed tomatoes

- 1 can coconut milk

- 1 bag fresh water cress

- Salt and pepper to taste

Directions:

1. Place the canola oil in a casserole. Add the onion and a pinch of salt. Wait until it turns translucent and releases its juices. Add in the potato, sweet beet, and pinch of salt. Cook for another 5 minutes. Then add the curry powder, brown sugar, ginger, and garlic. Stir continuously for a minute. Finally, pour ¼ cup of vegan broth. Use a wooden spoon to scrape the bits off the pan. Remove the casserole from the stove and set aside.

2. Into a slow cooker, pour the rest of the vegan broth, beans, bell pepper, cauliflower, crushed tomatoes, salt and pepper. Stir well. Cook on low heat for 7 hours.

3. After 7 hours, add the coconut milk and fresh water cress. Cover and cook for another half hour.

4. Serve and enjoy.

Healthy Mexican Fajitas

(Makes 4 servings - Cook Time: 4 hours)

Ingredients:

- 1 large white onion, sliced thinly

- 1 green bell pepper, cored and sliced into strips

- 1 yellow bell pepper, cored and sliced into strips

- 1 red bell pepper, cored and sliced into strips

- 1 tbsp. olive oil

- 2 tbsp. sliced jalapenos

- 1 tsp. smoked paprika

- ½ tsp. coriander powder

- 4 medium tomatoes, quartered

- Salt and pepper to taste

- 4 pcs. corn tortilla

- 2 tbsp. fresh coriander, chopped

- 4 tbsp. salsa

- 4 tbsp. grated cheddar cheese

Directions:

1. Put the onion, bell peppers, olive oil, jalapenos, paprika, and coriander powder in the slow cooker. Season with salt and pepper. Cook on high heat for 1 hour.

2. After an hour, add the tomatoes. Cook on high for 2 hours.

3. Place about half cup of cooked vegetables on a warm corn tortilla and top with cheese, coriander, and salsa.

4. Serve and enjoy.

Chinese-Style Broccoli and Tofu
(Makes 4 servings - Cook Time: 4 hours)

Ingredients:

- 2 packs firm tofu, drained, pat dried, and cubed

- 1 c. vegan broth

- 2/3 c. light soy sauce

- 1/3 c. brown sugar

- 1 tsbp. Sesame oil

- 4 cloves garlic, minced

- ¼ tsp. red pepper flakes

- 1 large head broccoli, chopped

- 2 tbsp. cornstarch

- 4 tbsp. cold water

Directions:

1. Brush the bottom of the slow cooker with sesame oil.

2. Place the dried tofu, broth, soy sauce, sugar, sesame oil, garlic, and pepper flakes. Cook on high for 2 hours.

3. In a small bowl, combine the cold water and cornstarch. Add the mix to the slow cooker and stir. Cook for another half hour on high.

4. Serve and enjoy.

Stewed Beans

(Makes 5 servings - Cook Time: 5 hours)

Ingredients:

- ¼ kilo white kidney beans, washed and drained

- ¼ kilo Great Northern beans, washed and drained

- 1 large carrots, peeled and diced

- 1 large potato, peeled and diced

- 2 stalks celery, chopped

- 1 white onion, diced

- 3 cloves garlic, minced

- 1 bay leaf

- 1 tbsp. Italian seasoning

- 5 c. vegan broth

- 1 can crushed tomatoes

- 2 c. water cress

- Salt and pepper to taste

Directions:

1. Soak the beans in tap water for about 3 hours. Rinse and drain the beans.

2. Place the beans in a slow cooker. Add the carrot, potato, celery, onion, garlic, bay leaf, Italian seasoning, salt and pepper. Add the broth. Mix well. Cook on high for 4 hours.

3. After 4 hours, remove the cover but do not turn off the slow cooker. Add the tomatoes. Season if needed. Cook for another hour.

4. Serve over a bowl of steamed rice or flat bread.

Bean and Mushroom Tacos

(Makes 6 servings - Cook Time: 2 ½ hours)

Ingredients:

- 1 ½ c. white kidney beans, washed and drained

- 200 g. button mushrooms, chopped

- 1 tbsp. canola oil

- 1 tsp. butter

- 3 cloves garlic, minced

- 1 tsp. cumin powder

- Salt and pepper to taste

- 1 Roma tomato, seeded and diced

- 1 white onion, diced

- ¼ head lettuce, shredded

- 1 c. grated cheddar cheese

- 6 pcs. corn tacos

Directions:

1. Pour canola oil in a non-stick pan. Add the butter. Cook the mushrooms for about 5 minutes. Stir constantly.

2. Add the onions. After a couple of minutes, add the garlic. Once the flavors have been released, add the cumin and then the beans. Season with salt and pepper. Stir well.

3. Transfer the mushroom mix to a slow cooker. Cook on high for about 2 hours.

4. Place a couple of tablespoons in each corn taco shell. Serve and enjoy.

Vegetarian Sloppy Joes
(Makes 5 servings - Cook Time: 6 hours)

Ingredients:

- 1 tbsp. olive oil

- 1 carrot, peeled and diced

- 2 small red onions, diced

- 2 cloves garlic, minced

- 1 tbsp. chili powder

- 1 tbsp. apple cider vinegar

- 1 tbsp. red wine

- ½ c. red kidney beans (soaked for a couple of hours)

- 1 small green bell pepper, seeded and diced

- 1 c. tomato sauce

- 1 tsp. tomato paste

- ¼ c. vegan broth

- 1 tbsp. light soy sauce

- ½ c. whole kernel corn

- 1 tbsp. coconut sugar

- Salt and pepper to taste

- 5 pcs. brioche buns

Directions:

1. Sauté the onions in a non-stick pan. Add the garlic and carrots after a couple of minutes. Add the chili powder while stirring constantly. Turn off heat and then add the red wine and vinegar. Scrape the bottom of the pan to get all the smoky flavour.

2. Brush the bottom of a slow cooker with oil. Place the drained beans in the slow cooker. Add the green bell pepper, tomato sauce, tomato paste, soy sauce, and broth. Mix well.

3. Finally, pour over the sautéed vegetables. Do not stir.

4. Cook on high for 5 hours or until the beans are tender.

5. Serve in brioche buns with a side of corn and coconut
    sugar.

Veg-hetti Sauce

(Makes 6 servings - Cook Time: 8 hours)

Ingredients:

- 1 white onion, diced

- 4 cloves garlic, minced

- 1 large carrot, peeled and diced

- 1 red bell pepper, seeded and diced

- 1 zucchini, diced

- 1 c. button mushrooms, chopped

- 1 can diced tomatoes

- 1 c. tomato sauce

- 1 tsp. tomato paste

- ½ tbsp. dried basil

- 1 tsp. oregano powder

- 1 tsp. dried thyme

- 200 g. spaghetti

Directions:

1. Place all ingredients, except the spaghetti, in a slow cooker.

2. Cook on low heat for 8 hours.

3. Cook the spaghetti in a separate casserole 30 minutes before the timer of the slow cooker ends.

4. Serve and enjoy.

Thai Vegetable Red Curry
(Makes 4 servings - Cook Time: 7 hours)

Ingredients:

- 1 c. low fat coconut milk

- 2 tbsp. Thai red curry paste

- ½ tbsp. organic peanut butter

- 2 c. vegan broth

- 1 tbsp. palm sugar, grated

- 2 small red onions, diced

- 1 green bell pepper, seeded and diced

- 2 c. pinto beans, washed and drained

- 1 carrot, diced

- 1 knob ginger, grated

- 1 tbsp. light soy sauce

- 1 pc. red chili, chopped

- 1 tbsp. fresh lime juice

- 1 handful lemon basil leaves

- 1 kefir lime leaf

Directions:

1. Combine the red curry paste, peanut butter, and coconut milk in a food processor and pulse until smooth. Transfer the mixture to a slow cooker.

2. Add the other ingredients, except the leaves, into the slow cooker.

3. Cook on low heat for 7 hours.

4. Stir in the basil and lime leaves.

5. Serve on a bowl of steamed rice. Enjoy.

Mexican-Style Quinoa

(Makes 4 servings - Cook Time: 5 hours)

Ingredients:

- 1 c. raw quinoa

- 1 c. frozen green peas

- 1 can chickpeas, washed and drained

- 1 large red bell pepper, seeded and diced

- 1 large tomato, seeded and diced

- 1 large white onion, diced

- ½ tbsp. cumin powder

- 5 cloves garlic, minced

- 1 ½ tbsp. prepared salsa

- 2 c. vegan broth

- Salt and pepper to taste

- Fresh coriander, chopped (for garnish)

- 1 c. grated cheddar cheese (for topping)

Directions:

1. Brush the bottom of a slow cooker with oil. Place the raw quinoa, green peas, chickpeas, red bell pepper, tomato, onion, cumin, garlic, salsa, salt and pepper. Stir the ingredients well.

2. Add the vegan broth. Cook on medium heat for 5 hours or until the quinoa is cooked.

3. Serve topped with cheese and garnished with coriander.

Mango and Basil Dessert
(Makes 5 servings - Cook Time: 2 hours)

Ingredients:

- 2 ½ c. all-purpose flour, divided into 2 equal portions

- 1 ¼ c. white sugar, divided into 2 equal portions

- 2 tsp. baking powder

- ½ tsp. cinnamon powder

- 2 organic eggs

- ½ c. almond milk

- 4 tbsp. olive oil

- ¼ tsp. salt, divided into 2 equal portions

- 3 whole ripe mangoes, peeled and cubed

- ¼ c. rolled oats

- ¼ c. fresh basil leaves, chopped

Directions:

1. Combine one part of the flour, sugar, and salt in a mixing bowl. Add the baking powder and cinnamon powder. Slowly add the eggs, almond milk, and olive oil. Stir using a wooden spoon.

2. Coat the bottom of the slow cooker with oil. Pour in the mixture.

3. In another bowl, combine the other part of flour, sugar, and salt. Add the mangoes and basil. Fold the mangoes in to be fully covered. Carefully add these in the batter in the slow cooker.

4. Sprinkle over the oats.

5. Cook on high for 2 hours. Check whether it is completely cooked by doing the toothpick test.

6. Serve with a scoop of ice cream or yogurt.

Banana Bread
(Makes 6 servings - Cook Time: 4 hours)

Ingredients:

- 2 organic eggs

- ½ c. vegetarian butter, room temperature

- 1 c. white sugar

- 2 c. all-purpose flour

- 1 tsp. baking powder

- ½ tsp. baking soda

- ½ tsp. sea salt

- 3 whole overripe bananas, mashed

- 1 c. dark chocolate chips

- 1 c. pecans

Directions:

1. Mix the eggs, sugar, and vegetarian butter in a mixing bowl. Add the baking powder, baking soda, flour, and salt. Whisk well. Slowly add the flour. Continue to mix until the batter creates a full consistency.

2. Add the mashed bananas. Mix again.

3. Finally add the pecans and dark chocolate chips.

4. Brush the bottom of the slow cooker with oil. Pour the mixture evenly.

5. Cook on low heat for 4 hours or until the bread is cooked.

Strawberry Lime Cake
(Makes 4 servings - Cook Time: 1 ½ hours)

Ingredients:

- ½ c. all-purpose flour

- 2 tbsp. granulated sugar

- ¼ tsp. baking powder

- 1/3 c. almond milk

- 1 c. strawberries, sliced

- 1 tsp. flaxseeds

- 2 tsp. warm water

- 1 tsp. olive oil

- ½ tsp. lime zest

- ¼ tsp. vanilla extract

- 2 tbsp. lime juice

Directions:

1. Brush the bottom of the slow cooker with oil.

2. Combine the dry ingredients and wet ingredients in separate bowls. Then slowly add the wet ingredients to the dry. Whisk well.

3. Transfer the batter to the slow cooker. Make sure the batter is evenly distributed.

4. Place a damp towel on the slow cooker before sealing the lid. Cook on high for an hour. Add another 30 minutes if the cake is not yet ready. Do the toothpick test to be sure.

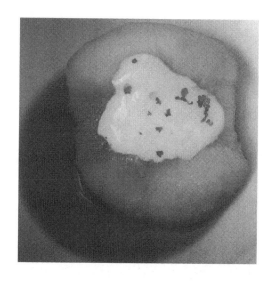

Poached Apples

(Makes 6 servings - Cook Time: 2 hours)

Ingredients:

- 6 Granny Smith apples, cored, peeled, and halved
- 1 tsp. cinnamon powder
- 2 tbsp. vegetarian butter
- 1 ½ c. brown sugar

Directions:

1. Place the butter, sugar, and cinnamon powder in a slow cooker. Place the sliced apples, coating each half with the sugar mix.

2. Cook on high for 2 hours.

3. Serve with a scoop of vanilla ice cream or yogurt.

French Toast

(Makes 6 servings - Cook Time: 7 hours)

Ingredients:

- 6 organic eggs

- 1 c. almond milk

- 1 tsp. cinnamon powder

- 1 tbsp. washed sugar

- 1 tsp. vanilla extract

- 6 slices whole wheat bread

Directions:

1. Combine the ingredients, except the bread, in a mixing bowl.

2. Dunk each bread slice in the mixture.

3. Place each bread slice on the bottom of a greased slow cooker.

4. Pour the remaining mixture over the bread slices.

5. Cook on low for 7 hours.

6. Serve and enjoy.

Conclusion

It is so easy to use a slow cooker. Just combine the ingredients together, set the time, set the heat level, and the slow cooker will do the rest. With just a simple kitchen appliance, one can prepare a variety of vegetarian meals. From soups, roasts, and even desserts, the functions of a slow cooker is limitless with a creative cook..

Use your slow cooker to bond with your families and friends. You can simply load the ingredients in the slow cooker and come home with a good vegetarian meal to share with friends. Your kids' friends can also have slumber parties without having to order pizza because you can prepare lasagna and apple pie using your slow cooker. The option is limitless when you have a slow cooker. Encourage your friends and families to invest in one and try the recipes in the book.